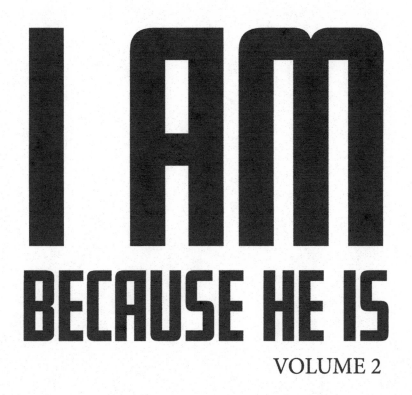

I AM
BECAUSE HE IS

VOLUME 2

Zavonda Vinson Parrish

ISBN 978-1-66783-713-0

DEDICATION

I dedicate this book to the brokenhearted, the secret keepers, the underdog, the untitled, the black sheep, the ones who pray but don't think God hears you, the lonely, the confused, the mother who may have lost her children to abuse or bad decisions, the addict, the alcoholic, the abused and used, the ashamed or maybe you got it all together. *I am proof there is a savior.* If you just hang on, help is on the way. God is a forgiving God. *I love you, but he loves you more!*

PROLOGUE

This volume will explain volume 1, and it will consist of different events that happened to me in my life. I've come a mighty long way; I've made many mistakes in my life that have indeed created this author. I'm not looking for anyone to pity me; I pray that the reader, in fact, can learn from my mistakes and change for the better. Many of the chapters may make one angry, sad, or even make one say, "how could she?" or "why would she," but to answer that, we've all got stuff! I did a lot of things, and even though I'm not happy about them, I did them, and I won't let that stop me from trying to help someone else not make the same mistakes I did or to help them get free of the ones they have made already. I've hurt a lot of people in my life, and if I've hurt you, *I'm sorry*. I can't explain why I did some things, and I may not remember, but I pray you can forgive me.

James 5:16, Confess your faults one to another, and pray one for another, that ye shall be healed. The effectual fervent prayer of a righteous man availeth much. Amen.

Volume 1 is my confession of my faults. I kept a lot of secrets that were destroying me and my family, especially my oldest daughter, physically, spiritually, and mentally. I wanted the world to know what I did and what I hid; even though this could have just been a private apology, I felt she deserved one publicly. I would have done just about anything for her forgiveness. A lot of things were swept under the rug, and if my prayer is to become a generational curse breaker, I have to start with the truth!

Matthew 16:19, I will give you the keys of the kingdom of heaven, and whatever you bind on earth shall be bound in heaven, and whatever you loose on earth shall be loosed in heaven. Amen.

PRAYER FOR THE READER

Father God, in the name of Jesus Lord, I come to you as humble as I can, asking you to bless my brother or sister who is reading this. I ask you to give them clarity as well as vision, Lord. I ask you to open up their hearts as well as spiritual eyes to see you and the works of you in this book, Lord. I ask you to answer unanswered questions and prayers. I ask you to heal their bodies as well as their minds, Lord. Show them who they are in you! Show them that with you, *all things* are possible if they only believe. Lord, give them a special touch from you on my behalf in the name of Jesus. Amen!

CHAPTER 1

Understanding

Many of you guys are familiar with the African proverb "it takes a village to raise a child," right? It's indeed *not* scripture; it was written by Jane C. Fletcher. But I do believe it to be true because children look up to others, whether it's a friendship or a relationship or just somebody other than a parent, but it does carry a scary side. Giving your child the "ok" to talk with someone else opens up the door to rebellion, especially if the child is talking to someone that has beliefs you may not agree with. So, even though I believe it takes a village, make sure your village is on the same page as you.

> Proverbs. 22:6, Train up a child the way to go, and
> when they get old, they will not depart from it. Amen.

So, even if the village you don't agree with gets a hold of your child, your child will have knowledge that is scripture when they are older.

Growing up, I could talk to my parents, but I didn't have much to say. I just went with the flow. I had feelings that I didn't know how to express, such as needing affection. For example, my mom and grandma hugged and kissed me and told me they loved me, but my dad didn't, so I wouldn't know how to talk about that; I just figured that was just him, not knowing it would scar me for life. My grandmother's side of the family spoiled me big time. I grew up thinking everything could be bought, even friends. If I cried, my granny bought me something, and it made me happy, so if someone I cared about showed me they were sad, I gave them something, and it made them happy. So I figured that was the right medicine, and that grew with me. I'm telling you this now; if this is something you are doing, *stop it now*. If you think you *can buy* love, you can't. You can surely buy some time, but eventually, it will run out. If someone loves you, they won't take advantage of your kind heart. Pray and ask God how you can help without giving everything you have away so that people will love *you* as a human being and not just for what you do for them.

Ladies in a relationship, it's ok to show your man how to love you. Many of us think "they should know," but how would they? Half the time, we don't know ourselves. Many of us walk around stressed to the max because we want affection in the relationship. But think about this, we express our needs through anger or silence, and who is just going to hug and kiss an angry, quiet woman? Sis, it is ok to say, "I need to be held or hugged," if he loves you, he will do it. Most men do exactly what we ask anyway. Also, daughters, say to your dad, "I want to hang out and hear stories about your childhood," or just "say you want to get to know them," or ask about their favorite things (I'd give anything to do this with my dad). Nine times out of ten, you will find their sensitive side in conversation, and that should help you guys open up. Daughters, tell your mom how you feel. If affection is what you need from her, tell her. Write her a letter if you feel uncomfortable talking at first. Even though they are your mother, they don't know everything. Help them love you guys better.

1 Corinthians. 13:4-5. Love is patient, love is kind; it does not envy, it does not boast, it is not proud. It does not dishonor others, it is not self-seeking, it is not easily angered, it keeps no record of wrong. Amen.

CHAPTER 2

Communication

Communication definition means of sending or receiving information.

Many of us are still trying to find out who we are, but I can guarantee you will find out who you are not first! Communication *is* key; even though I found that to be true later on in life, *it is true.* Communication comes in five forms: verbal, nonverbal, written, listening, and visual. I've failed at all five! I could very well be talking while writing, hearing but not listening, and looking slam through you all at once. You get it, lol. I'm serious, but I encourage you to find out how well you communicate and comprehend yourself and others. I'll explain; I am a very hyper person; I get excited fast, and that causes me to be very loud when I talk. My voice is deep, so I intimidate people when I could very well be just talking about how to cook noodles. I didn't realize this at first. I would find myself in arguments after arguments, and I never knew why, just by asking a question. Also,

I have a 9th-grade education, so my grammar is way off, so that affects the way I communicate as well. I may ask a question that sounds like an answer, so that would confuse people too. I pray you are following me, I'm going somewhere with this. I realized I was being misunderstood when I was told, "I hate talking to you because you YELL too much." Hmmm. So can you only imagine how many people, even my children, ran away from talking to me? I used to say, "I wonder why my daughter didn't tell me what she was going through," but I'm sure she was scared of my response. If all I did was yell, she was scared to talk, and how could I blame her or anybody? I now explain to people how I communicate, and it seems to help people understand me. No matter how old you are, evaluate yourself and see what you can do to demonstrate your character better.

> *2 Corinthians. 5:17 Therefore, if anyone is in Christ,*
> *the new creation has come. The old has gone; the new*
> *is here. Amen.*

When I got saved, it was like God handed me a mirror and as bad as I wanted to see everyone else in the mirror, he showed me *Me*. I was pure hell on wheels. I never ever liked to resolve anything; I always suppressed it. One of my favorite lines was, "it's all good Ima be ok." Does that sound like you? Think about how many times you have said that. If you had a brick for every time you said it; I'm sure you could build a small house, maybe even a big one. Pushing stuff to the side is never good; it's ok to take a breath if needed but resolve it. Never leave it alone, especially if it bothers you. *Deal With* It. If you don't, the issues will come back to you even if it's ten years later. The way I communicated in the past is affecting me now; God has truly humbled me through my pain as well as the pain I've caused others. Once he showed me the pain I've caused, I vowed I'd never hurt anyone again if I could help it. I now look for ways to better myself. The more I seek to be humble; I become A NEW CREATURE. God hears your cry even if you are trying to cover up something; He knows all. While you are waiting on Him, He is waiting on you!

CHAPTER 3

Experience

Have you ever said, "I love all my children the same."?

I did, and saying that showed me exactly why I didn't know what I was saying. My children are, in fact, my children, but they are all different, and loving them the same is impossible. I was going through different stages of my life during each birth; having my first child, I was a child myself, my body wasn't even developed, so she raised me. I had no clue how to be a mom, but I did the best I could with the resources I had. If I can explain the levels of my maturity on a scale of 1-10, I was a 3. All I knew was that I had to feed, bathe, clothe, and protect this child, but only if she was hurting. I checked on her if she cried, I knew that was a sign that something was wrong, so if she didn't cry, she was fine, so that's what I knew. I also knew I was going through hurt and betrayal from her father, and trying to raise a child with a broken heart is not healthy. I was 15 years old at this time. I was in love when I first had her, and to find out she had a brother still in diapers devastated (even though I stayed) me. Can you imagine how I felt when I looked at her? All I could imagine was some guy hurting her the way I was hurt. I did not want that to happen to her. At that moment, I started raising her out of fear and a broken heart. I was planning her life to be bad before she could walk. As she got older, I never wanted her to talk about a boyfriend. I would always talk as if that was the worst thing ever. I fussed about education being the main focus, something I knew nothing about. I confused that child big time. I was clueless myself; all I knew was that I didn't want her to get hurt, but I was teaching her exactly how. I showed her tough love at an early age; I wanted her to be strong-willed at the age of three. I used to make everything a punishment; thinking back, I used to scream, "wash the dishes, clean the house, watch the kids, do your homework," cheer all in one breath. I never asked how her day was. Really, I was like a drill sergeant when I was only trying to teach life skills. I made her hate what she was supposed to use. When she got older, I never really gave her hugs and kisses; the same affection I lacked in return caused her to lack, and I did that with each of my children. For the longest time, my son got the more affectionate parts of me. I raised him opposite. I didn't want my girls to turn into me, and I didn't want him to turn into the guys that hurt me. It's taken me going through all of this to realize I was going crazy and thought I was ok (*check on your strong friends and yourself,* just because you think you're ok doesn't mean you are). It's one thing to have a child at an early age but to try and raise them by only what you feel is the worst! Message to mothers: having your heart broken will make you live in fear. If you have a son and a daughter and have been hurt, ask yourself, are you doing something similar to what I've done? I truly believe some of us parents force our kids to like the same sex by pumping fear into them early about the opposite sex, instead of showing them that love is a good thing if it's *love*. Had I waited until I understood what love was, my life would be different. My intent was never to hurt my children's feelings, never. I never wanted to hurt them, period, even though that's what happened. *Hurt people hurt* people.

Self-awareness is important; it's up there with *communication*. Do you know you? This may sound weird, but in self-evaluation, I've figured out that I don't really like all that hugging stuff. I like to hear *love*. I *liked* to be told how much I am loved, or buy me something that looks like love, and in return, I gave that. What I lacked was verbal affection. I hugged my kids sometimes, and I may kiss their foreheads, but that's what I like. I liked to give gifts; I liked to see their faces light up when they got that thing I said I wasn't going buy while acting like I was mad. I liked to tell people how I feel, mostly by showing them. Some parents like to hug and kiss and show their affection that way, and it doesn't mean I loved my children less; it's just that I gave what I liked, and I'm finding out that may not be enough for some people. I was never able to explain this until later in life, when I realized I mattered. I asked myself, "what do I like?" Relationships are ending because of stuff like this. Evaluate yourself and explain it, and if someone tells you they need you to hug them a little more, it is a thing called compromise; that's a new word I use often. I pray I'm helping someone.

Proverbs. 4:7 Wisdom is the principal thing; therefore, get wisdom: and with all thy getting, get understanding. Amen.

CHAPTER 4

RIP

RIP is usually a phrase people use when someone dies, but it's now a phrase I use daily. *Rest in Peace While I'm Alive.* That's all I crave; living a lie has got to be the most frustrating way to live ever. You have to stay away from certain people just so you don't have to talk about certain things. I made the church my safe place; I could go there and scream and cry, and people would never really be concerned about the real problem; they would always say, "God will fix it." And even though He will, I was glad no one asked me to tell them my reason for saying hallelujah.

CHAPTER 5

Vulnerable

For the love of a man, a woman will do just about any-thing. I was sober when I met my first child's father; I was also a virgin. He was older than me; I remember overhearing my older friends' conversations about guys not wanting a girl that's a virgin. I was so green I went out and had sex with a guy I cared nothing about just to be ready for the guy I wanted. I thought I had to be experienced to date an older guy. After my daughter was born, I used to drink a beer here and there. I wasn't old enough, but I needed to fit in. I was very-weak minded, but people thought I had it all together. My daughter's dad went to prison, and I started hanging out more. One beer turned into drinking wine, turned into drinking liquor, turned into smoking weed, and that's when the door was opened for a different crowd which led me straight into a relationship that would have me trying cocaine to keep my man at home! Yes, I tried it; I thank God I didn't like it because I probably would be dead. Sure enough, I remember even contemplating taking a charge and possibly going to jail all because I loved a man. I did so many things I didn't like; I ate food I didn't like just for the sake of being called "my everything." I look back at all of that stuff, and I say, "God, you kept me, and I thank you!" what if the cocaine was rat poison? I didn't know what I was doing what, if it killed me; I was so young, but God, *he Kept Me*. All for the love of a man. Many may say they wouldn't do certain things, but I've also talked to many that have tried things just because of their significant other. I also talked to some that do things and don't recognize why they do it, and they turn their nose up as if they are perfect. We as women should never have to lower our standards for a man, but how do you know if you are lowering them? When you believe you're in love and they love you, you become weak, and your decision-making is based off of how strong they make you feel. What are you doing to keep your man? Are you keeping secrets? What have you done to keep a man? Answer those questions for yourself. Like I said in the beginning, you will find out who you *are not* before you find out *who you are*. It's a lot of kids being had out of sneaky link relationships then we get mad when the father doesn't want to be involved. All for the love of a man, you will even bring a child into the world knowing it's a 50/50 chance he's going be in the child's life, so again, I ask, what will you do for *Love?* God forgave me for that, too; I'm just trying to help someone get free.

Give your life to Christ; let him use you. He's the only man I know that knows all of your secrets and will still love you unconditionally.

CHAPTER 6

2012

My stepson's death hurt me; here I had been asking God to take me away, and my stepson's life was taken by an accident. The day of his death was a crazy day; I was drunk, but I could. My then-husband and I were arguing really bad; that was normal, but this day I just felt that I wanted to leave, and I meant to leave for good. I didn't feel like I was going to die, but I had made it up in my mind if I had to die, I wanted to go with

God. I packed a bag of clothes, and I clutched my bottle of liquor, and I headed out the door. When I got behind my steering wheel, I remember telling God, "if I die, I want to go with you, God." The sun shined so bright it was like a sign from God saying, "I heard your cry." I left my home, and I got on route 360, walking distance from the funeral home, and the traffic was backed up. I was angry because I didn't want to wait, my phone kept ringing; I finally answered. It was my stepson's mother wanting to know if the boys made it safely to bring my son his gifts for his birthday. I told her, no; not knowing that it was the boys in the accident that was holding up the traffic. It was then I found out that they were preparing to remove the driver's body out of the car, and the lane would be open for us to get through. As I began to look, I kind of recognized the back of the car; it looked like my stepson's girlfriend's car. I got out to go see, and I was grabbed by a gentleman that knew. I knew the driver, and he told me the Baker boy didn't make it and the other son was being transported to the hospital. My heart dropped; all I could think about was that I had to go home and tell my then-husband that his son was gone. After that, I sobered up, and I felt that I didn't want to live the life I was living anymore. My childrens' hearts were broken; I lost my daughter the year before to the system. They were granted custody, and now this. I just wanted to figure out how I could fix my family, so that's when I tried Jesus for real.

Being saved happened through confession; if you haven't been saved, read this prayer: Romans 10:9. Confess with your mouth *Jesus is Lord* and believe in your heart that God raised Him from the dead, you will be saved. Amen.

I got saved, but I struggled with being sanctified (that's being cleaned up). I was saved but still drinking, lying, and overall, sinning. Sanctification is the stage everyone thinks they can just clean up by themselves, then come to God. When In all you need God to even go through that stage it's going to take many scriptures and prayers. One scripture that helped me was:

Lamentations 3:22~23. The steadfast love of the Lord never ceases; His mercies never come to an end; they are new every morning, great is your faithfulness. Amen.

That Scripture let me know that I probably would fail at some things, but God gives us another day to get it right. And a lot of prayer.

1 John 1:9 if we confess our sins, He is faithful and just to forgive us our sins and to cleanse us from all and righteousness. Amen.

I screamed out for God to help, literally, *"God, it's me, I need you!"* I told God my problems and stuff started falling off. Everything happened over time, not overnight. Sometimes I prayed and didn't get an answer right away; yes, I got discouraged, I got frustrated, I got angry, I backslid, I even doubted God at times because I wanted him to move when I said it, but it doesn't work like that. You have to wait. It's a time and a season for you, for everything,

(Ecclesiastes 3). You must wait for your season. It's going to get harder before it gets better, but it's the process, trust it. Just continue to seek the Lord; He will come through!

CHAPTER 7

Exposure

I often asked God, "how did I get to the place I was at?"
I was a normal kid; I liked to play kickball and basketball, I liked to play
Nintendo, I liked to draw, I liked cartoons, and I loved to eat candy. I was
just a kid; I didn't like to be looked at; I used to skip past boys in school so
they wouldn't look at my butt; I wore baggy clothes and all. It was when I
got exposed to sex at 14 that my life changed forever. Once something gets

woken up, it's hard to put it back to sleep. Having these conversations with your children is important, don't let the streets teach them. You will know when the time is right. Talk to them, tell them that being touched inappropriately by anyone *is not ok* ever! Being exposed to anything too early can be detrimental. Even though my kids know just about everything about me now, they can never tell you they saw me do anything in front of them. They never saw me smoke weed, nor roll it. They may have smelled it. Even though I didn't do a lot of things right, I didn't do drugs in front of my kids, nor did I let them see me with other guys in an inappropriate way. One bad decision caused a snowball effect of bad decisions for me. Tell your kids you love them, tell them they are beautiful or handsome, tell them they are stars. I believe that this should start at home and even if it's too late, your children may be grown, sit them down and tell them about you. It may help them. Getting it off of your chest may help you as well. Families have secrets; no one knows what goes on behind closed doors, and definitely not in the mind of a broken woman.

CHAPTER 8

Comprehension

I spent 20 years crying and depressed, not wanting to share in Father's Day, my Dad's birthday, or holidays. I would rather work than spend time with my family. Not really understanding what I was experiencing, I am now learning about grief. There are six stages of grief: denial, anger, bargaining, depression, acceptance, and then reconstruction. And grief doesn't have to be for someone that has lost someone due to death; you can grieve a person that you once loved, like a marriage ending in divorce or just a long-term relationship ending. I'm sure that pain is worse than death when you can still see that person, and they moved on with someone else. I was married, and I didn't get married thinking I would ever lose my husband ever. My child's love, I never would have guessed we would be going through something that could cause us to not be under the same roof for years. My dad died; he was supposed to walk me down the aisle; how could he die before he had seen me happy? I remember when my dad was alive, I used to be so angry with him for the way he treated me in my first book; even though I forgave my father for putting a gun to my head, I hated him and wished him to go to hell for a long time. So, when my dad died, I felt guilty for feeling that way about him; not able to say I was sorry, I blamed myself for his death.

> *Proverb 18:21 The tongue has the power of life and death, and those who love it will eat its fruit. Amen.*

Be careful what you say, it could very well haunt you years later. I didn't want my dad to die, I was just angry, and we all say things we don't mean. I encourage you to *think before you speak*! I was in the first two stages of grief denial, and I was angry; for years. Denial, who wants to believe any of this is happening to them? And the more I thought about it, the angrier I got, which caused me to bargain, with alcohol, drugs, and meaningless relationships that made me depressed, never dealing with anything I went through because I felt like I lost already. Volume 1 caused me to realize I've never *grieved at all*. I just suppressed everything when my dad died. I was in a very dark place, I was living in Richmond, I had no car, I was pregnant, I was lonely, and I had no plans for my future yet, and again I was pregnant. I had nothing, but as soon as he died, I woke up to everything, two cars, money, two houses, but still no plans for a future. No one ever thinks someone is going to die and put you in that position, so I wouldn't have planned how to live when I'd rather have been dead. My dad's death saved my life. It literally *saved my life*. Even though I was sad, I was happy. I could breathe. I felt like this was my second chance. I felt it; I wish I understood that having a counselor was ok. Even though I believed in God, He puts people in place to help you (if you think you need to talk to someone, *Do it*.) I needed someone to help me process my pain; I needed help finding the root of all my pain and also to understand that I needed to deal with stuff one pain at a time.

Habakkuk 2:2. Write the vision make it plain on tablets so that a runner can carry the correct message to others. Amen.

If you are going through something, write the vision of yourself being *free.* Whatever that looks like, manifest it.

Write the vision for your marriage, for your family, for your health, and your wealth. It's not just about business; it's about your way of living as well! Pray, write, and pray again.

The year 2021 was better for me. Through all of the pain I've caused and pain I've felt, I accepted the fact that I couldn't change everything I've done or gone through; I only could apologize and repent.

CHAPTER 9

Forgiveness

How did I forgive?

Colossians 3:13. Forgive as the Lord has forgiven you.

Matthew 18:22 Up to seven times but up to seventy times seven if anyone wrongs you keep on forgiving.

Forgiveness has to be hard when you have to forgive someone who never says they are sorry, right? I'm telling you, it's hard, but it's possible with Christ! The more I sought, the more I wanted to forgive. That's when the seventy times seven comes in; it's healing in forgiveness. When I forgave my ex-husband, and I forgave myself, God allowed me to release volume 1. God knows I wanted to behead him, I did not want to forgive him at all, but I would have only become a victim. I believe that he has a chance to get saved just like I did. Forgiveness is deep, it allows you to search into your soul, and it makes you compassionate for others, not for the person's flesh so much, but for their soul. It makes you pray for them on a level you would pray for yourself, and God knows when it's sincere, so don't think you can just say it and not mean it because you will be tested. Trust me; I knew I had forgiven him when I was willing to pray for him and to give him a plate when he was hungry. That's growth, that's forgiveness, that's God!

How did I forgive myself? And how did I know I was forgiven? I acknowledged my part, and I forgave myself, first for not knowing, I forgave myself for not understanding, I forgave myself for being, I went through the majority of my life just winging it; if it felt good, I did it again. Right or wrong, I lived mainly off of feelings. I've wronged a lot of people. I've thrown rocks and hid my hands for years. I'm not better than anyone, but if the Lord forgave me, I surely could forgive myself! Even though I don't regret anything I have done, I do wish I could have explained my reasons for doing things better. My mistakes have made me into the woman I am today. I know God forgave me because He says He does in His word, but it's a feeling of relief you can actually feel when a burden lifts when you go to God in *all truth*. I mean *all truth*. You can feel the freedom from it, you can feel the fresh start! You have to hang on to that and understand that just because God forgave you doesn't mean the people you've hurt will. Think about the pain you've caused and how long it took you to admit you were wrong. Think about the process you had to go through, and don't get mad if they don't forgive you yet. Apologize *and mean it*, and give them space. Don't force yourself on anyone; it could make the situation worse, but indeed keep getting better. Keep changing for the better; keep showing fruit. Forgiveness is an action word, don't go back and do the same thing you asked someone to forgive you for. Even though they may not say it, they are watching. Time heals all wounds; give it *time*. The Bible says in 1 Peter 5:7, Give all your worries and cares to God, for he cares about you. Amen. Pray for them to obtain a heart to forgive and trust again because forgiveness is for them first.

CHAPTER 10

Reconstruction

Hurting my oldest daughter scarred me. The child that I once couldn't figure out why she loved me so much. Eventually, she told me she hated me, and I understood. It made me shy away from parenting my other kids. I never wanted to hear those words again. I've let them make decisions on their own so if they failed, they wouldn't blame me, and I'll be darned if I wasn't told by one of my other kids, "I wish you would tell me no." I'm understanding that you will be damned if you do and damned if you don't; we as parents have to just be honest and stern, practice what you preach. My dad never saw me saved, but my mom did. She showed me how to continue paving the way for my children regardless of if they are listening or not. I was hardheaded, but she kept praying, and look at me now, my kids are hardheaded, but I'm still praying. I'm sure one, if not all four, is going to write a book one day about their lives. I'm just going to keep laying down the pages, so even though this journey has its ups and downs, it's going to be all worth it. I'm leaving a legacy behind. I encourage all to stay humble, keep God first, pray for strength and understanding; you will need it. We are raising children that are media-fed, even some of us parents are media-fed. Please make sure your foundation is on the word of God, introduce Christ to your children and all who will listen, not just by words but by your lifestyle. Communicate, and make sure everyone comprehends. No two people are alike, and that's ok; pray for patience; before you judge someone, talk to them. Conversations can close wounds that stitches can't. Be kind. Even though I believe this hell part of my life was supposed to kill me, God knew it would save me; the devil has to ask permission.

> *Job 2:6 Satan hath permission to afflict Job, but the Lord said to Satan, "very well, you can do what you want to him but spare his life." Amen. In other words, you can't kill him!*

I put myself into that scripture, "you can take Vonda for a ride, Satan but you can't kill her. She belongs to me," and for that, *I give God glory! Though they slay me, yet I trust God!*

> *Job 13:15 Though he slay me, yet will I trust him: but I will maintain mine own ways before him. Amen.*

(song for worship) The Potter's House by Tremaine Hawkins

Get to know God yourself!

Job 42:5 I have heard of thee by the hearing of the ear: but now mine eye seeth thee. Amen. My mom has taught me everything about God, so I "heard" about Him through her. I used to be so afraid of Him and anything connected to Him, but I always listened to the stories she told me about Him. One story she told stuck out the most to me, I was young, and my mom used to be a smoker; she loved Salem cigarettes, and one day, she asked God to take the taste of cigarettes from her, and He did it! She never smoked again. That stuck with me. I later on figured out that was called deliverance. I used those exact words when I got delivered

from alcohol Lord, take the taste out of liquor away from me, and He did it. That's when I knew He was real, that's when my eyes seeth him, that's when I wanted to know him more. If He did that for me, what else can He do? Many people haven't experienced an encounter yet; my prayer is you see Him for yourself.

I AM TOOUKY products...

Website: www.iamtoouky.com

Email: iamtoouky@gmail.com

IG: @i_am_toouky

Dreams do come true…my first billboard.

I AM ZAVONDA

Healed people help heal people!

Special Thanks:

My reason, Lynesha, my oldest daughter; She's my reason for change, and even though our relationship is not where either of us wants it to be, I'm not going to stop changing. I'm not going to stop evolving. Time heals everything; it has no limits to what you can and will do. You are very creative, stay that way, and I love you.

My Angel Tyjion (Bug), my son, I call you that because you are. You saw me struggle, and you stuck by my side, and that's something I'll never forget. We talked about hope often, and that's what gets me by. Hope never lose hope, Son. I don't know what the future holds but if you want it go for it! I know you will change lives through your lyrics I AM SURE thank you, Bug for everything; I love you!

My Challenge, Endia. Lord Jesus, the one that gives me a run for my money, but I truly appreciate you. Your realness, no matter what, stay honest, stay a leader. I'm proud of the young woman you are becoming; thanks for listening to me cry; I love you!

My Wake-Up call, Tracie (Toouk). You are such a smart young lady, and your generation has woken me up even more. It's made me more determined to want it right! At least leave knowledge, understanding, and wisdom. I'm going to leave you the torch with that old soul; Jesus is the only way; make sure you tell the world when I'm gone; I love you!

MANY WILL SAY

THE END,

BUT I'LL SAY

THE BEGINNING!